From the Farm to the Table Almonds

by

Kathy Coatney

Copyright @ 2014 by Kathy Coatney

www.kathycoatney.com

From the Farm to the Table Series
From the Farm to the Table: Almonds
Book 5

All rights reserved

No part of this publication can be reproduced or transmitted in any form or by any means, electonic or mechanical, without permission in writing from Kathy Coatney

CONTENTS

Dedication . . . . Pg iv

Acknowledgements . . . . Pg 1

From the Farm to the Table
Almonds. . . . . Pg 3

Vocabulary . . . . Pg 27

Lesson Plan . . . . Pg 28

Author Biography . . . . Pg 33

Dedication

Thanks to Farmer Dan for his time and expertise.

Acknowledgements

Many thanks to those who have assisted me with this project. Georgia Bockoven, who put the idea in my head. To my email check-in pals, Jennifer Skullestad and Lisa Sorensen, a huge thanks. Luann Erickson, Susan Crosby, Karol Black, and Tammy Lambeth, who critiqued and supported me through the process. To the Redding Lunch Bunch, Libby, Shari, Diana, Lisa, Terry, and Patti, you're the best. To my family, Nick, Wade, Jake, and Emily. You four have been my inspiration. Thank you. I never would have made it without you.

Note to parents and teachers: The underlined words are second-grade vocabulary words. A list of the words used can be found at the end of the book along with a list of almond industry terms and debate topics

From the Farm to the Table Series

From the Farm to the Table: Dairy

From the Farm to the Table: Bees

Pizza, Tacos and the Olive-Fingered Kid

Spuds, Taters and the French Fry Kids

From the Farm to the Table: Almonds

Farmer Dan

Farmer Dan is an almond guy. Almonds are a kind of nut that grows on a tree.

Almond Hull

Almonds have two outside coverings. One is the <u>hull</u>, which is green and fuzzy. Inside the hull is the <u>shell</u>. Both protect the almonds while they are growing on the tree.

Each February, thousands and thousands of tiny, pink blossoms cover all 500 acres of Farmer Dan's almond trees.

Farmer Dan puts two beehives on every acre. The bees fly through the orchard and <u>pollinate</u> the blossoms.

Farmer Dan says, "Bees and almond trees need each other because they have to work together to make the almonds."

Before and after the almonds bloom, the bees need food, so Farmer Dan plants wildflowers around his almond orchard for them to eat.

Farmer Dan says, "You can help feed the bees, too, by planting wildflowers."

Almond blossom being protected from frost

All through the bloom Farmer Dan watches the temperature closely. If it gets too cold he has to <u>irrigate</u> to protect the almonds.

Tiny almond growing

The blossoms begin to fall off the tree after about two weeks, and itsy, bitsy nuts begin to grow.

Farmer Dan <u>inspects</u> the almond trees regularly to make certain they are healthy and produce lots and lots of almonds.

Farmer Dan's almond trees work really hard, and each tree produces about 20 pounds of nuts per tree, which is approximately 2,500 pounds of almonds per acre.

Almonds being harvested with a pole

Before almonds were harvested with machines, Farmer Dan used a long pole to knock the almonds out of the trees. Today he has all kinds of machines to harvest them.

Almond shaker

Farmer Dan uses a <u>shaker</u> that clamps metal arms around the tree trunk and shakes the trunk so that the almonds fall to the ground.

Windrow

Farmer Dan leaves the almonds on the ground to dry for 7 to 10 days. After they are dry, he drives a <u>sweeper</u> that puts them into <u>windrows</u>, then he scoops up the almonds with a tractor pulling a <u>harvester</u>.

Almond sweeper

The fan on the sweeper blows dirt and leaves off the almonds, creating dust as thick as fog in the orchard. Farmer Dan has to squint to see through the haze as he drives the transporter full of almonds.

Almond transporter

Farmer Dan dumps the almonds onto a <u>conveyor belt</u> that loads them into a bigger trailer.

A truck hauls the almonds to the <u>huller</u> where they are dumped into <u>big</u> 25-foot-high piles. That's four times as tall as Farmer Dan!

Conveyor belt

At the huller, the almonds are loaded onto another conveyor belt that Farmer Dan says looks like a long winding road. The fuzzy hulls and shells are removed from the almonds by machines.

Almonds being processed at the packer

Farmer Dan says there are all kinds of almonds. Some are processed raw (uncooked) and others are roasted in big ovens in a variety of flavors.

Farmer Dan loves almonds because they are packed full of protein that grows muscles and provides energy, plus they have vitamins and minerals to build healthy hearts.

Almonds are Farmer Dan's favorite snack. He <u>especially</u> loves how they crunch when he eats them.

Almonds being put in cans

Farmer Dan <u>prefers</u> his almonds raw, but he also likes them flavored with honey Dijon. What is your favorite almond?

Almonds are a lot of work, but Farmer Dan loves raising them from teeny, tiny baby nuts to full grown almonds.

The End

Vocabulary Word List

Big
Especially
Inspect
Prefers
Squint

Almond Industry Terminology

Bankout
Conveyor belt
Harvester
Hull
Huller
Irrigate
Packer
Pollinate
Shaker
Shell

Sweeper
Transporter
Windrows

Author's Note

The following pages include information on the almond industry for creating a lesson plan. This information is also available on my website and Facebook page. I will continue to add information, so check for updates, or sign up for my newsletter on my webpage, www.kathycoatney.com, for all the latest information.

California Almond Production

Almonds are grown throughout California's Central Valley which stretches nearly 500 miles. The top almond producing counties are in Kern, Fresno, Stanislaus, Merced, and Madera. In Fresno County (2014 figures) for instance, almonds are the top crop with an estimated value of $772,616,000, followed by dairy at $503,540,000, livestock $498,041,000, raisins $467,280,000 and processing tomatoes $365,750,000.

Almond varieties

More than 40 varieties of almonds have been developed and grown commercially. The most popular varieties of almonds are Mission, Price, Carmel, and Nonpareil. Most varietal research today focuses on developing varieties that are more resistant to insects and disease. Almonds are related to the peach and rose families, and most almond trees are grafted to peach rootstock which is more resistant to pests.

Almond production

California is the largest supplier of almonds in the world, producing approximately 80 percent of the world's almonds and 100 percent of the U.S. commercial supply. The U.S. is the largest consumer of almonds, and China is the largest importer of California almonds, more than 168 million pounds in 2010/2011. Other importers of California almonds include China, Germany, India, United Arab Emirates, Japan, Canada, Turkey, the Netherlands, and Italy.

California Common Core Standards
Jargon specific to the almond industry:

Almond grower—farmer
Bankout—vehicle that hauls almonds
Conveyor belt—an automated machine that moves the almonds
Harvester—picks up the windrows of almonds
Hull—the outer covering of the almond
Huller—removes the hull from the almond
Packer—packs almonds into containers
Shaker—a machine that shakes the almonds from the tree
Shell—the inner covering under the hull
Sweeper—a machine that gathers the nuts into windrows
Windrow—a long line of piled nuts

California Common Core Standards
Ideas for Almond Debate

Are almonds good for you?
Which is better, organic or non-organic almonds?
Is urban encroachment dangerous to agriculture?
Would you want to be an almond farmer?

Other Topics for Debate

Should agriculture or housing be in flood zones?
Who gets irrigation water?
Should everyone be allowed to drill a well?
Should water be moved out of its county?

Websites for additional California almond information

Facebook for teachers and parents
https://www.facebook.com/fromthefarmtothetable

Data per County for top five Agricultural Commodities
http://www.cfbf.com/CFBF/CountyFarmBureaus/CFBF/CountyFarmBureaus/Default.aspx

Almond Board of California
http://www.almondboard.com/Consumer/Pages/Default.aspx

University of California, Davis, Almond Production Information
http://fruitsandnuts.ucdavis.edu/pages/almond/

Author Biography

Kathy Coatney has worked as a freelance photojournalist for 20 years, starting in parenting magazines, then fly fishing, and finally specializing in agriculture. Her work can be seen in the California Farm Bureau magazine, *Ag Alert*, Farm Progress' *Beef Producer* magazines, *West Coast Nut Guide* magazine and *TimberWest* magazine. The From the Farm to the Table children's stories are her latest project.

View her photos at: www.agstockimages.com
Like her at: www.facebook.com/fromthefarmtothetable
Follow her on twitter @kathycoatney
Visit her website at: www.kathycoatney.com

Made in the USA
San Bernardino, CA
28 November 2016